playland

poems 1994–2004

playland
poems 1994–2004

by
eve packer

Fly By Night Press
a subsidiary of
A Gathering of The Tribes, Inc
New York

FLY BY NIGHT PRESS is a subsidiary of A Gathering of the Tribes, Inc.

COPYRIGHT @ 2005 BY EVE PACKER
playland
poems 1994-2004

ISBN 1-930083-05-X
Library of Congress Control Number: 2004096733
printed in Canada
some of these poems have appeared in *cafe review, excursus, JumpArts Journal, Long Shot, Mudfish, Nuyorican Poets Cafe* (Zurich), *Oral. Paramour, Poetry in Performance, No roses review, Tribes, Verbal Abuse*

thanks to the Chester H. Jones Foundation National Poetry Competition Commendation, the National Endowment for the Humanities, and to *Time to Consider: the Arts Respond to 9/ll* Award

Huge thanks to: David Trinidad, & Susan Sherman, Danny Shot, Steve Cannon, & to: Greer Goodman, Donald Hall, Noah Howard, Chris Marchetti, Gregory Nagy, Stephney Williams, David Wechsler & Ms. MercyB, MPHC, the crew at Tribes, the 42-4st gang, and most of all, ny, ny

layout & design: laraine goodman (hella@mindspring.com)
cover & inside graphics: robin hendrickson with alexis cook
nyc photos: eve packer (evebpacker@aol.com)
author photo: john ranard

Fly By Night Press
PO Box 20693 New York NY 10009
tel: (212) 674-3778 Fax: (212) 388-9813
email: info@tribes.org
www.tribes.org

to doris, my mom,
leo, my dad, &
for sam, my son

CONTENTS

Author's Note

how the 'times square' poems got made: I remember it was winter
& really cold. For years, every day on my way home from teaching
uptown i would stop off and swim at my health club on w. 43rd st.
This meant walking past the area bordered by 42nd to 44th streets,
from times square to 9th ave. I happened to see a small newspaper
article saying disney had bought up a lot of property around 42nd
st. this was the early 90's. And so i knew the area was about to
change.

It also occurred to me, that, even tho i walked by these 'peep-
show' places, and although most of the workers were female, that
it was a world forbidden to other women. I suppose the idea of
walking thru that closed door intrigued, scared, and challenged me.
I decided to risk going thru those doors. And i also decided that if i
spoke to the women who worked there i would ask them some
'big' questions, about life, love, their points of view. I always paid
for the interview. I wasn't allowed to carry a camera or tape
recorder, so i would talk for one minute—the exact time the
'peepshow' window stays open for one token. Then i would rush
outside in the cold, and write down the conversation. I also took
some photos which are part of this investigation, record, memory
of that time and place.

What amazed me from the start was the willingness, even eager-
ness, with which people answered my questions—my feeling is it
was the first time any woman had walked in and asked about their
thoughts and feelings while they were on the job.I always began by
saying, 'my name is eve & i'm a poet.'

I guess some would call it a sleazy world, but it was most indi-
vidual, particular, theatrical, fleshy, moving, and often funny, fun. I
was treated very well, except the first time, when i was thrown out
of Show World because i lacked a male escort. After that, i moved
up the avenue to Peepworld, and Playpen; I also spent a certain
amount of time at Sally's, the world famous transvestite bar and
showplace, opposite the *NY Times*.

I was right, of course, the neighborhood did change, i guess, for
the better, yet like the song says, 'but not for me.' Show World is
now the Laugh Factory, tho some version remains next door,
Sally's became Club NY, scene of the infamous Puffy-Shyne
shoot-out, its now closed; Lingerie and Blarney Stone are now the
Hotel Westin. I miss the flamboyance, the vitality, that life, that ny
life, the ny world that is so much a part of me.

atocha

every time i
do the backstroke,
head up, facing
        the blue sky
& manhattan plaza tower, i see
the building falling
& the bodies, bricks
crashing thru glass,
blood
in the
water

i dont remember
atocha station
but i sure remember
the prado
&

hieronymous bosch,
who pre-saw the fire,
demons, twisted forms,
dancing deaths wreckage,
& goya & the horrors

of war, the paintings
live, but
atocha station is blasted, boneyard,
today all the papers
carry the photo of thousands

of spaniards protesting
the 3/11 attack umbrellas in the
frame to frame
rain—& spilling out
of the frame—

more bodies, carnage
yet to come, quick look
at the bosch! visions
of hell and humans morphing
to skeletons & death heads

hokey-pokeying in the fire

                                        3.12.04

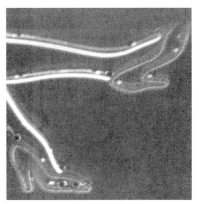

fantasy booth

show world

is the showpiece
of 42nd st, a cross between
penn station & a brothel:

the marquee reads:
show world center
XXX movie
    25¢
live nude revue

Triple Threat Theatre
the zipper runs:
live-sexy-girl
girl-shows
cozy-warm-comfort-tonite-live-

in front: two
video screens: a large long-hair
brunette w/white dress
huge tits: offering bliss
w/her smile

the sign on the plexiglass:
MAC
Master Card
Visa
you must be 21 yrs

of age
no drugs
alcohol
food
1 to a booth

intoxicated or high persons not permitted
no woman admitted w/o male escort

Fun & Fantasy
    25¢

cecil on the deuce
(1)

ebony is 5'11"
beautiful body
blonde wig
right abdomen:
old cig burn,
right deltoid:
cut-scar

shes working her way
thru pharmacy school
at l.i.u. stripping
down behind the glass
door, doing what you
ask for — $10 bucks
& up —

at showworld

    water/
    sky/
    fall
    down/
    part of
    earth/
    to
    grind
    up/
    crush
    heart
    mesh
    flesh

      a
      true
    bird journey

lisa has stretch
marks, and when she
turns her ass, massages
her labia, you can see
shes had an episiotomy,
can move the muscles
of her vagina lavender lipgloss
nails — slip 2 bucks
thru the slot —

the window comes down at playbox video

murdered bird
girl
thats my
rain name/
all hands
 to me/
so when do
i go

true
sun
water
moon i love you
i like you
gonna go
see you
bye

Love
Labia!
— Eve
xoxo

(3)

      in the hall a man in camel
hair coat & gold rim glasses
asks if you wanna share a video
booth

       no thanks

stargrit in yr
fingernails
      semi-naked
females at their doors:
nookie court, jam yr logs up
my hole, ca ca doo doo —
strip/girl/strip (strip/girl/strip)

the man with a mop is very busy

     the bell

    mercury mist

    single marimba
note/
so swan
so far
some wind

(4)

short hair blonde
riding big dick up her ass
up and down up and down as many bucks as as you can shell out
replay the video

does it hurt asks my escort, a doctor

ass riding
the cushion/ horse-hair tail
wave-jasmine tea
shoulder
& labia

> grunt to the
> overbite/
> deal/ deal
> deal
> or die
>
> fight/ hand
> foot/ blind
> freaky
> eye

(5)

Did you see the old woman–
the homeless one
& the strung-out bleach blonde
on the phone
albert pouring murphys ale
and that john eyeing me
did you see the way
the hooker grabbed
the pimps crotch him assbackward
legs up in the air

     dreaming in colors/
     skin silver vinyl/
     lick
     candle mesh
     honey
     a voice on the phone
     so relax, hips a
     bracelet, stars an
     eye, skin this
     candle
     sunrose
     wind
     down

(6)

slim, white levis
black sweatshirt, hair sliced
up in hot pink elastic, groovin
movin to the beat, hooked in
to her walkman, hip & shoulder,
arms & feet, wedding ring, one
tooth in upper lip

very slim very high cheekbones,
very stoned, smack of course,
& AIDS

ex-go-go dancer, still got
the moves of a movie
star

    spirit
    god
    black as river blood
    bright as glitter foil
    spattered sun sun
    my word
    an
    eye

pediatrician, scrawny, army
fatigue jacket, stringy pony
tail, goes w/yasmin, TV out
of l.a., putting her thru
electrolysis school, he says:

80% of the girls here
over 30, 35 are HIV positive...
out on the street
at 12, 13...they cant
go home...

& the first ten years
are an up, lotsa money
rolling in, living w/
an older queen, showing
them how its done

most of them never use
their dicks...
then theyre 35—if theyre
alive...then what...
i dont know...they become

alcoholic...or...
cracked by angel light

    snake
    river
    time
    down where
    the nile life
    is near
    yr
    sin/begin

    down where the nile life is near yr skin
    begin/time

next door at lingerie

hanging underbrush,
square fluorescent grey cube,
silk sateen underpants, dildos,
lacy bras and frothy camisoles, mesh stockings
w/o crotch, whips & chains, oil & glitter

on a shelf behind glass
a cardboard box reads Lov E-W-E: the
party sheep: inflatable: the friend youve
always needed love you have
always dreamed of—the little lamb
you can love & will love you back—

in this grey fluorescent box of wild dreams,
schlock fantasy, backstage for the suck & fuck
school of sad & horny fish:

warren, the skinny salesman in eyeglasses
& striped shirt, his skin
very pale lets me take notes:
cause i buy 1 pr of purple 100%
cotton bikini briefs (4.95)

guy in fedora coked to the max
picking up ben-wa balls
for his girl: i ask him
                    what do men want
                    he says *freedom, freedom*
                        & a little variety

i say: is that what you tell yr girlfriend

at sally's

sylvia del rio is stacked
& sits at the circular bar
in her long black spaghetti
strap dress, long bleached auburn
hair, cats-eye mascara, wide
& gorgeous mouth: a whiff of
drive-you-wild in-your-face
perfume & performance: tossing
·her head, shrugging a shoulder,
arm on my arm, leg on my leg:
ava gardner, sylvana mangano, raquel
welchoverblown & hot: *i'm a pre-op*
transexual (she writes in my book):

> *a (she-male) is someone*
> *that looks like a woman*
> *but rally a fagit*

> *(transvestite*-spelled *travestie)—someone*
> *who is a hard hard*
> *man who fantasize at*
> *being a woman*

> *(pre-op transexual):*
> *someone before she chop off*
> *her Dick*

in july she broke up with her boyfriend:

he doesn't
pay homage
anymore—i'm a queen—he's a liar—getting fat
missing a tooth—lazy—

what wld make you happy?
stiletto dropping a dime, hard as nail
hitting bulls-eye she says:
someone to share my life,
appreciate me—if

you can't do
that—

yr a piece of shit—
give me
my trophies

you're out–
             as i go she tells me her phone number:
you can suck
my dick
anytime—

round &soft & full moon,
ny times clock reads: 6:34,
very warm for january

fantasy booth: ebony's rap

"bob he says his name is bob
so i keep my panties on then take
them off a little, rub up & down,
is your cock in yr hand i say,
is it hard, he says he wants
to rub whip cream
all over me, lick it off,
i rub my tits
& clit, say bite it, he says
he wants to kill me, bite it
i say, pushing my clit in his face,
give em a little then pull
back, its all abt giving them
some & pulling
back, i put my face real
close to his like this/he thinks
im really gonna put my tongue in his
mouth
                give me a
                break

i go up real
close, im getting so excited
i say his hand on the glass
rubbing my titties
jerking off w/the other,
im making my sounds, oh i say
oh oh, oh he
says i came
you came i
say/you
ruined my
fantasy—"

peepworld (1)

monique is naked
& big/phony
red dreads/shaved
pubic hair

whaddya do i say
if you gonna get
  a guy out
  fast

legs splaying the
universe, pushing
pussy in my face,
she starts rubbing, stop, enuf

I say, what else—
let em suck
my titties
shake my ass

window comes down:
transaction: time: 60 seconds
                cost: 6 bucks
 5 for her, 1 for the house

old man
at front
glued to
box video (Blondes & Blacks starring Kayla

Kleavage) spooning bean soup
from blue
    paper cup

peepworld (2)

diana, curly hair, mega-friendly, hoop earrings,
hanging w/gina, slinky high-cheekbones
from philippines, chewing
on licorice, orange lips dangling
cigarette/midriff half-up to show
small flat breasts

when i ask do they jerk off
gina says, *all the time,*
but you don't pay
attention

she & diana
chorusgirls on
line chime:
its just a job
come back

peepworld (3)

roxy tilts back her head,
arms, kimono black long
hair flung out, rocking a little

at the open window where two
hands , one on each breast,
are rubbing, round & round

for each new customer she says:
tip & touch
tip & touch

peepworld (4)

pebbles (outta staten island)
turns ass hard
in my face shakes,
bends over
front, touches
tits:

some of em touch,
some of em watch,
she motions down
here, *jerk off*
> *most these*
> *days just watch*

cause of AIDS

peepworld (5)

what do you wish for
the new year:

at the cash register
tom from sri lanka says:

harder work: in the back,
the three women:

chipmunk (the bronx):
better tippers

gina (philippines):
big dicks, more sex

carolina (dominicana):
men treat us better

window down
on peepworld '95

the song is:
open yr heart

2 take 5

narrow bed

                      string of beaded stars/
                      lamplight/fire
                      light/yr eyes

blueblack flowers
under sea
drifting/shifting

face facing me

mural at minton's

museum

i live in NY and do not wear
a wild painted feather
amazon headdress

in my cupboard i carry no
small shelf heavy
with cowrie shell skulls, ritual

swords, bells, and tiny wood,
stone, or clay figures, no false-face
mask or sekire inhabit my history

no beaded kachina dolls, batik cloth,
olmec heads, jaguar necklaces, straw or beads
or painted clay, no gourds or fabulous bows

or gold crown

my legacy is a feather pillow
used for barter in odessa streets,
a torah, of which i know nothing,

a few lost words, shayna maidle,
yartzheit, baruch atah,
                    femished, fablonged,
                    fahtootzed, facachta,
a faded recipe for blintzes

grandma left me, my legacy is
a concrete bunker
bronx gutter, and the sound of a single

sax at the corner, jagged & warped
as city wind, my legacy
is billie & sidney & louis & bix,

dad mixing up the paints, mom wielding the brush
in a circle of ice and fire, no yiddish in this house, or hebrew
just the sound of glass cracking as

daddy screws another woman, punches
mom in the stomach, belly blue,
in front of me

writhing monkey on the bathroom
floor, like the stuffed specimens
in these cases, who is there to talk to

books lots of books and visits to this
museum where the enormous whale hung
in strange spirit light—

i have cravings, i have desires

to carry colors of earth
on & in
me

& sometimes i do

percy

sledge singing when a man
loves a woman, how many
times have i heard

it, riding
on the back (the pareja) seat
coming from a *bembe en habana*

la vieja, someone blasting
his voice from one of those
sumptuous old buildings on

avenida la quinta, girls
lining the road, & before that
long ago, how it rips you up, how

every woman wants those words
that gut-splitting beat

#36

  POLICE knocking &
we just in the door, POLICE knocking,
fortunately the door is just this sec
shut, we are not yet in flagrante, but
fully clothed, tuned into what i'll later

tag our song: the weather station: #36,
"room 904 or 902" says the short fat mustache pig-
let when you open up, "report of domestic violence"
& we are just the prime suspects he is
in search of, nicole & oj, but mini, much

cuter & smarter: "i'm an artist, officer" you say,
"oh" he says "must be the other room," we can hear
voices, "she's hiding in the stairwell," sounds of
tense confab, handcuffs (unclear), before
the footsteps have passed, we're at it,

mutual consent i remember you sd in the
street, i thought you were nuts, but see why,
well yeah, i'll consent to this, anytime any-
place, any universe or niche, day, night, quantum leap
rolling steaming typhoon thunder, monsoon

& tidal wave, lightning-bolt flash, its
a hit asleep, in arms unarmed, i hear in hall,
sound of leg, metal stump, capt hook, phantom
of sid & nancy, rapping & tapping,
what grade b horror flick creature is

here, fortunately you put a chair in front
of the door how illogical its locked, i think,
if you can call it thinking, breathing
free, so far gone, easy

swept away

after we do everything,
every filthy, nasty, sweet
thing, after you face me,
deep, deeper, in some unknown
place, after riding my back ancient
warrior thunder-lightning desert rain
smashing naked skin, after you come
in me, after taking my pussy from
the back, after me sucking yr dick
again, again, after all that, blue light
morning air, you put yr head on my chest,
ear to heart, say, tell me a story mami mami tell
me a story...

Hale-Bopp

You got YR
dick so far up
me its
in mouth
exploding out
my soul dont stop
you say
if i pause
or rest
    dont stop
      ·i keep
        hip stuff
moving
you moving in
me
  toes curling
burning corners of map, scorching
the torches, comets falling thru orbits
& galaxies you riding me grabbing
my hair, hand to nape of neck, naked nightrider,
bareback on whirlwind, rearing, screaming,
falling wet in me, a kiss, peace

for a minute

drifting deep into sleep
               holding me close you say
closer, slo-mo, fastforward, pause, where
is time & who
am i

Hale-Bopp
appears once every 4200 yrs, we spot it
from the prow of staten island ferry hurtling
the waters back to manhattan, our
turn now

mural at minton's

                      for erica

i'm thinking of the long deserted room,
wood floor, brick walls, the unused
refrigerators, old costumes on hooks, the
busted xerox, bare light bulb

& at the end of the room, the mural at minton's,
the wood around it painted green, at the center
a window of brown-black sky
one star

on the left a big brass bed, & the figure
on the bed, face down, is a woman in a red
dress, all we see is her back & long black hair,
they say its billie, is she nodding, or just flinging her hair
to the cool white sheets

on the right a wood dresser, from the top drawer
hangs a sock, on top a kerosene lamp, an ashtray,
lit cigarette, some matches, maybe, &
the four musicians

one sitting on the bed playing a horn, i dont
remember him too well, except his dirty blonde hair, on a chair
up right the trumpet player, hair conked & parted, eyes lowered,
or maybe thats the guitarist,

you can see the sand & smell the turquoise
sea, the jacaranda hibiscus in the air near
where hes playing, & the drummer is using *the daily news*
for sticks to keep quiet cause its night,

at their feet a little white dog w/black patch,
looking up—at the star, the open window, the music,
the sky, the mural is signed
charles graham '48

i remember i used to go on my break from work,
after seeing my student who lived across the street,
& died at 21,
when she was 9 her head & legs got bashed

against the wall so bad her dad was sent
up for 2 1/2 years,
ms. p she'd say *dress for the weather,*
carry an umbrella,

you'll get wet

twisting fingers

for pennies,
whistling in
dark, the dark
an aura,
a hay-
seed jumpy
rhinestone
bloom,
so what you
say,
so here
how gone

the girl in the red dress is me

this dress in so short.
from paraphernalia
in ny/ I must be 19.
we're in madrid. the
poet & me. madrid,
so hot, so terrific.
shrimp & tapas.
lotsa traffic, people
tons in the streets—
its noon like that
& we're walking,
heading up on the
concrete, & this truck,
the truckdriver calling
out to my skirt, my
reddress my legs me,
the truck goes rightup
on the sidewalk & hits
the wall

/paris

i can see them walking,
strolling from chatelet to
gare de nord, pre-dawn, few cars,
fewer people, shuttered charcuterie
& brasseries, metro shut, &
theyre carrying instruments, in what
is called the tone zone, rapping
music, old stories people
they know, who owes them money,
no place to get coffee, sit down,
no train to take, finally at 6:30,
one can get the metro, the other,
no francs, train, food, just
a horn, sitting back to closed cafe, looking
at huge statues on gare de nord, waiting,
dawn & its blue

photo op
for sam

renaissance angel,
imp, sun/shadow
botticelli
in garden, someone
i'm most proud of

travels across the
world to meet
her, comes back from difficult
trip w/this
memento

of what
they call
    a
lyric
moment

wanta tell him:
women like that,
elusive, abt to dive
into water or disappear,
are dangerous, but

only to ourselves

canto

after i got off
work today &
before i hit the
pool i took
time to
sit on the stoop
in the sun
(1st time since
early fall)
black coffee in
white paper cup,
hard wholewheat
roll in
hand
& thought:
how much
easier it is to
describe someone
who works in water,
words or wood
than Loremil
who worked in
air space & fire...
all i
know is when
he put on his
whites/under
the spotlite
at s.o.b.'s:
in a capoeira duel:
the gods came
down—
now like
the snow in
central pk he's
gone:
fri nite at
columbia-presbyterian, age 40,
so they say, of AIDS

easter bonnet

in yr house there is no god, so the rules get broke
(in secret), an xmas tree (very big), and
bread at passover (mom sends you to the store,
shes too ashamed), & at easter, the parade up the concourse,
patent leather shoes and brand new straw
hat, velvet ribbon and fake pink and blue yellow
flowers—what rules here:
        moms paintbrushes, daddy jazz, their bed, breuer
chairs, bruises on her belly, picasso rug, arms skin
broken silk—
        breaking the rules, as madonna sd
last night on letterman, what else
is there—

but of course it is difficult to walk naked in the
easter parade nothing but yr straw hat and some
lovely fresh flowers, noone wld notice, or they'd
call you crazy, i remember the story abt

georgia o'keefe screaming cause a niece caught
her painting naked in the garden—
naked and gleaming
        cellophane melted wax under a

    painted moon

voice

hes whispering in my ear, in a language,
in words syllables & sounds, i hear but
dont understand but i do, & hes got an indio
face, hes abt 17, maybe, a wood indio
face, & hes pouring words down
my ear, have some rum he says,
handing over a brown paper bag,
we're sitting on the front steps, i've just
finished fucking saying goodnight
to my boyfriend, an extraordinary
artist, his drawings are all over
my walls, i have that effect on him, come on
he says, taking me down the road,
                                         its a night
w/electricity, i know cause the
posada is open, he takes me down the road
thru the field w/long wild reeds first its
dark then we have the moon, hes carrying a machete
talking talking down my ear, no one has
ever talked down my pores like this wood demon
from a lost world,
kissing dark in the road, & at the posada by
the sea, but you cant see it, just the mural of naked
bodies by the door, & the bulletin board
w/reglas para los companeros para limpiarlo
& a room w/ 1 big bed & wood headboard, tile floor,
fan on ceiling, sink, toilet, and we throw
off what there is of our clothes, & come

I'M A NY WOMAN, I DO WHAT I WANT

do not tell me what I cannot & can do

do not tell me to wear long black baggy pants
when I wanna wear a short sheer orange
see-thru mini on subway, bus, tram, train,
trolley or any vehicle/of choice

(thats in moving violation of my volition/do not tell me what I
cannot & can do)

do not tell me not to bite my nails,
color my hair, ride my bike
w/o helmet, stop giving taxi drivers
a hard time piece of my mind,
cross against the light, (why
else is it red), sit on someone elses
stoop, swim twice in one day,
eat so much fruit
do not tell me what i cannot & can do

do not tell me not to talk to
strangers, flirt, network my cleavage, keep my legs
crossed & mouth shut while you are
orbiting saturn
do not tell me what I cannot & can do

I pay my rent, con ed & phone, get to work on time,
health club, yoga & dance class (sure need my r & r after
this urban guerilla warfare), I light a fire
under my own stove, or use my phone-finger
for take-out, ticketron, 1-800, do not tell me
what I cannot & can do

& do not say you'll e-mail if you won't,
call when you don't, do not appear late, make or
change plans w/o consulting, promise then cop, say you love
me & get misplaced, love & 1.50 will get me on the 1,2,3,5,6,7,
A,C,E F,D,N,R or shuttle 24/7 this is ny if you love me baby
show up

& do not tell me I cannot start my song
w/cannot i'm a ny woman I do what I want,
do not tell me not to go to the deli
at 4 a.m. stark naked even if there is no deli

& STOP TELLING ME TO STOP MAKING NOISE

playland

playland

playland it was called playland hector valentine took me
well I guess I was 14 hector valentine used to sit in the back
                              of math class
throw spitballs you know he was tall & thin I just thought
he was cool anyway he took me to playland I dont remember
                              a thing
except we got pizza I vomited in the gutter—well I mean
you didnt go to 42nd there were whores

& pimps & thiefs & stuff, you didnt even look at
the neon cause it was just too dangerous to glance
at what it might be saying well a little later in spring
probably kurt who was black so I cldnt take him home
& he certainly wasnt gonna take me home we used to go
to the movie houses they were $2 they must have
been a dollar or less no they must have been a dollar

& sit up in the back row of the balcony & make-out cause
where else were we gonna make-out, I think we were totally
oblivious to the activities arnd us & they were probably
oblivious to us—before I see 42nd again
I was in college I was in europe then when I
came back

I got to be an actress & you just live
at 42nd I used to think it was so strange you know here you
are in this 'respectable profession' I guess you can see
its roots esp for women are definitely in whoredom cause thats
the district so there you are going to yr audition on those streets
in the w. 50's but you gotta walk by the 40's on the way to the

subway, & you sorta squinch yrself up make yr field of vision
                              tiny like
a mini-horse w/blinders so you dont see the secret shame
marquees but also so noone will see or hit on you before you
manage to get downstairs toss yr token in the slot
ride home & say oh no that place doesnt exist, oh no my life has
nothing
to do w/42nd—
                    playland—it was called playland—

eve

tread softly if you tread
on me, you tread on apple,
snake, eve

58

ego de philemm abrosun. [ ] *touto kai moi*
to lampron eros aelio kai to kalon lelonkhe– sappho

HABROSUN TO THE MAX, EXCESS, COURTING
danger, foot to the abyss this
& lust for suncircle burnt hibiscus aqua-
marine glitter necklace has won for me
toy in crackerjack box, long straw, gold in
stream, lotto ticket this for me
has won rainstorm i open the door to,
water spill/candle burn/
heart
wings
flame

pier

OCEAN eye
yellow & red
ferris wheel on mile-hi blue gypsy
sky
7 seas

*

watertowers black on pearl-grey,
black watertowers on sunset

*

dawn & dusk, dusk & dawn dawn
our time

*

white light late
            afternoon

*

                          floating
grey towers blinking
      tall lit ship

*

gold banner day
square root of blue

*

water fire & water
sea/sea & sky one
horizon line gone

*

carnivalcarnival all the time

*

ocean eye
yellow & red
ferris wheel on mile-hi blue/

my shoes is wrong

ACROSS THE AISLE
on the uptown c
this labor day
they're wearing adidas
& nikes, & 1 pr of slingbacks
in white trimmed w/black

down the next aisle
on the uptown c
at 12:30
they're wearing adidas
& nikes & 1 pr of jellies
in black trimmed w/white

my shoes is wrong, I got on
a pr of beige SAS sandals,
comfy as peanut butter bunny slippers,
but wrong

my shoes is not black or white
but biege & wrong wrong wrong

see/saw

i may not look like a see-
saw but thats who
i am. up/down/down/
up or i might be a jump-
rope running in circles a hoola
hot pink hoop—what a child—
i wish—thinking of what
my ex who i saw on the corner
this morning in front of chase
atm sd:

i keep seeing the hour glass running
out.

a soft-boiled egg

a soft-boiled egg is easier
& faster than a hard one, having no
patience, thats what im having
on the stoop

               hot & sweaty, hemmed
in by heat & concrete, air
thick as old sneaker, blasted
bell of our lady of perpetual

knuckleball, my soles
sticky gum on wheel of
life, want ice-cream
but its something-

else, want to escape blue
on blue. or maybe its just
my horoscope, this is a bad
bad afternoon

sitting w/my hard-boiled egg,
planning my next move

floyd

a raincloud of
gummi bears, bold
as the A train, new

as Fubu, penumbra
of blue, a raincloud of

gummi bears, place-
mats of light, all summer
we prayed for

rain, now we got
hurricane, beware of

answered prayers they say,
you're nothing but
trouble, you know how I love

thunder, lightning, flash-
flood storms, a raincloud
of gummi bears, penumbra

of blue, at this glitter-
fest oh what i'd give

to have you up here in my big
blue bed big piece of plastic/
top of construction site

whipping the
wind, ocean waves over roofs

t for trash

garbage is
bits of
stink broccoli.
fleas in the
litter, urine-
stained
daily news.
chicken & bbq
rib bones
crunch plastic
cups, spoons,
plates, cookies, olive-
oil paper napkins, take-
out
   Trash
is glitter-
soaked rain-
wet orange
day-glo tigerskin ripped
& torn pants,
tank-
tops, crushed lipstick
shoulderpads

   Someday
i'll be garbage,
   ash,

for now
tag me hard-core
   Trash

colette

        we're at the end of the time
when i can wear my gauze lightly,
send out my words in a
stream, twisting the chicken's
head so the blood runs free,
crossing the street against
the light, the minotaur in the mirror
is me, the minotaur
& the branding-
iron the sleek cat
ready to pounce

when

when the city
is like this night
fallen down,
when the city
is like this,
a few lit windows
in the
dark, when the
city is like this
night fallen down

cruisin' w/moxie

cruisin w/moxie

cruisin w/moxie
aka sexy scorpio ny fox
cruisin w/moxie
   no taxi
cruisin w/moxie

cheatin'

(1)

the advantage of living
on the 5th floor

you can step out the
shower stark naked &
dripping
wet by the time
the delivery kid is at
the door you're ready
for whatever
he got

(2)

fri afternoon &
we're shaving
our legs, prepping
for evening
ahead, parties,
who knows, getting
dolled up in
what? ripped
jeans, tight striped
t-shirts, stevens co-op, where
i first cooked lasagna, smelled
lilacs, fell in
love,
      young

i've cheated on every man but one,
  every man has cheated on me,
    more times than even i, long-distance swimmer, can count

(3)

jerry hall says living w/a womanizer
doesn't do much for yr self-
esteem

in the same *daily news* an
article abt jackie o. how she
sorta ironically said I dress

to attract men how jfk called
her the sex
object, tho he was the mack

in the 1st family, living
w/a womanizer doesnt do a lot
for yr self-esteem

& the phone calls, hang-ups, the side-
trips, finally jane becomes a christian
& turner apparently is devastated

you can cheat once, twice, lotsa
times, then
the rose-water is

on the floor the river
flowing
out the door

& how to put the pieces back

(4)

my heart is not
breaking

far from australia
& nicole kidman

no wiser tho
she says she is

blue sky doesnt
bother me, nor

the fact you say
youre running

around, nothing
bothers me

much but

(5)

dont let him
lie to you
  honey
cause you know
  he will
you know he will
dont let him
  cheat on
    you
cause you
  know its
  done
dont let him
rock her
  world all
night &
  say hes
clean
dont let him
  lie to you
  honey
cause you
  know he will
you know he will

(6)

telling a woman
to start cleaning
house is like buying
shoes for a man:

he'll walk
she'll throw you out

orula

i've only known one orula
keeper of dreams,
he sang abt mama africa, how
he had been working
in the fields & they
came & took him
from his love, they took him from his love

i've only known one orula,
keeper of dreams, he had a
chinese grandmother, & an african grandmother,
played drums, married
to a great dancer, she died,
leaving a strong
son

i've only known one orula, keeper of dreams,
he had the smoothest
skin (& greenest eyes) of any man
i've ever known, if you see him, tell him
i'm thinking of him & the terrace
by the sea, tell him
i'm thinking of his song

& how he danced w/his hat &
cigar, a glass of rum
to his mouth

what is love (1)

billy i say,

we are at Playpen, girls parading
plumed & feathered birds of
paradise, billy slamming tokens
right & left fistfuls
of peppermints, friday rush hour,
hi-5's, kisses from dancers to
frequent customers, in this semi-
naked arena billy i say what is love
& he puts it on the mike:

being one w/the one
you desire, you cld come in on
yr hands & knees, i'd throw
my arms arnd you, give you a
big kiss & hug, say thats
my baby, other people
wldn't understand
but i do

love, what is love i say to dillon
cop on the corner: *like*
parent w/a kid, like the
church says come hell or high
water

love what is love i say to candy the TV
he has just chased, the one w/
the terrible face job awful jaw stubble (i guess
this is her corner), what is
love: *caring for me, knowing what i*
do, this is my job she says
desperation leaking from

running mascara, *caring*
not abt what i do,
but for who i am

love i say what is love to rumanian
taxi driver: *what makes me the greatest*
fighter in the world, what is love i say
to my friend nancy: *wet underpants,*
what is love i say to bob
first warm day of spring looking up
coffee cup in hand he says
constant sunlight

      love i say what is love
      to the voice in
      my ear & you say
      what i'm waiting for
      you to tell me

down at the cooler (2)

under freon freeze lavender light,
what is love i say to wilber,
bass packed up, fez on head
he says (pointing to friends
at the bar);

               this—
this is love—
2-3-4-
 5-6-
  7

adds

early
morning
2 crows
mating in
 the
mist—

what is love (3)

peter says *jazz*

what is love (4)

        i say to my mom,
a shrug
      then
love is
hunger

what is love: husband & wife (5)

assif says:
an anchor in the clouds

suzie:
what i live for

what is love (6)

eyeliner perfectly applied,
egyptian style, bracelets in place, new
caribbean colored bathing suit,
dee back from the hospital says:

> *the*
> *quality of yr*
> *life is changed*
> *when he*
>   *enters*
>   *the room*

> *takes off*
> *his shoes/*
> *lies down*
> *next to*
> *me/in*
> *the emergency*
> *room—*

(6a)

what is love i say to miles
on the phone,
        just back from
europe he says—*pickled grapes*
        like when
        you drink too much

in the steam room, saturday (7)

naked, gleaming
      wet
   safe from cold,
      life
   men
   what is love
         luz
               (lifeguard
               playboy gorgeous
               20's)
laughs *too much,*
nina
               (choreographer
               therapist
               lady botticelli
               40's):

      i can only
      say what
      my mom says:
      god is love
      & love is
         sex

esther (60's):
      i agree
      but say
      love is
      lust

      women i say
      think that
      not men/
      not til

later says
nina/*by then*
esther says *its*
too late,
they're running
downhill
   well she
says, sitting
   up,
   at least yr
mother talked
abt love, mine
only abt marriage/
oh, nina
says, *my mom* (noted robotic physicist)
   wasn't interested
in marriage, she
only married
my father
cause it was the
only way
he'd screw
   her—

(8)

what is love
singh taxi driver
from india says:
some
love the self,
some love the
money, the body,
but the true love
who love
the soul

(9)

what is love

berne says:
midway between
passion &
duty

adds: *there's*
no casual sex
if its really sex
there are sexual casualties
but no casual sex

adds: *bridge*
            &
      tunnel

adds: *passion bridges*
the anonymity

(10)

selena singing a*mor*
prohibido on the jukebox,

up from ecuador, sitting
at sally's bar,

what is love
daisy says:

he picks me up after
work every day

(11)

what is love
noone asked me
but
love is
the one who
lights
the room

(12)

jeri
kissing close
at Playpen i *dont*
know/love/is a dream

out on street/2-tall dudes
rapping: michael (bouncer):

wow noone
ever asked me that question:

zigs when
its sposed to zag

i can see michael says *a woman*
in the dark (2 people laughing
during orgasm), a woman in the dusk, rose
in her mouth, tear down her cheek,
a smile

jonah (painter) says:
she just left town

87

(12a)

what is love
i say at *5C*
& vattel (lst time i meet him)
says
    another breath

(13)

what is
love
sam, my son says,
taking the $20,
love is
   impossible

outside

       its raining
been
raining all day
& its gonna rain
    thru tomorrow:
vivian behind
the bar always
behind the bar at sally's,
french chignon tastefully
arranged, lined
worn face, stolid sad grey
eyes, punched
out tooth,
bare-
back
sequin minidress,
fine legs in
black tights

what is love

depends she says:
theres love of things,
family love, sexual
   love
     i
dont know
its a feeling,
light, airy
  some people
 are scared

next to me
TV w/
high india cheekbones,
long black hair, wide
white smile/
    & Charlene tall
cindy crawford knock-off

what is love

money they
say
no money
no honey

vivian is thinking/
looking me straight
in eye she says/
i've had a hard
life/done a lot
of things /i love
children/scanning
the room/*i've taken*
care of a lot of children/the girls are talking
money & food:
              eggs mcmuffin
            baloney sandwiches
            fries & frito-lays
            shakes
            mcdonalds

i love
children vivian says
    sometimes you try
    to block
    the pain—

on the e train:
tall girl,
long brown
hair
carrying an
enormous bunch
of pink roses
wrapped in plastic

still raining at 14th st,
our umbrellas blow inside
out, 6:45, bitterly cold
may 16th, time to go home,
drop my things,
move on

window: 9/11

<u>9/11:9:05 a.m.</u>

2 explosions—
18 min apart:
while teaching
Ian: smoke billowing
Jet? accident?
doesnt seem possible—
            (illegible)—
   after 2nd:
what why?
hideous
people—
one of those—

9/11: 10:30 a.m.

in front of my window,
saying into phone:
the second tower just collapsed
before my eyes

right then the color
seeps out of my field
of vision, knees
go

smoke now white/grey
huge smoke on
perfect
blue

nite
without
sound, no
traffic

nite
total quiet

nite
eerie
quiet
no traffic,

no sound,
from time
to time,
chopper,
fire
siren
        in the
a.m.,
no birds
no birdsong
   south
of 14th

9/14: fri nite

candlelight vigil, front of
white horse & hudson corner cafe,
3 beefy undercover cops, one in
red white blue bandana, pony tail,
jump out of unmarked van, they,
we all, hold candles,
no traffic, no chitchat, silent

7 p.m. dusk just falling

pick-up truck passes
w/a load of ash-covered
firefighters, silent unmoving,
like that kids game: statues

9/14: st vincents hotline

fewer callers,
calls beginning to get thru from
overseas, and now the children
are calling, not tiny kids
but 10, 11, 12, you can hear
the baby crying, or the adult,
the kids the only ones who speak
english, or are calm enuf
to take down information
& numbers—& now for the first
time, and from a child i hear
do you have the morgue number, the
address of the morgue, theres
a little girl named amaryllis,
she calls twice, & i think
its amaryllis, i know a
child the
first to ask
is there a list of
the dead

<u>9/15: sat. a.m.</u>

out the window
shadow of some tree
i cant see, shadow of leaves
on back of small building

today is sunny,
blue sky, white cloud where
towers used to stand

used to be

instead of pulling
down the shade, i pull it up
for a minute
face the view

9/16: at the health club

leonardo, age 4,
red pants
sitting on the
ledge picking
his nose,
next time
are they
gonna fix it,
mom, are they
gonna fix
it next
time
& she, tying
his shoes,
i hope so

jumping down,
throwing towel
for cape over
shoulders, he's shouting
superman, i'm
alive, i'm still
alive!

<u>9/19: corner of nassau & liberty</u>

ground zero air
filthy brown
dust//
when you take
pics you dont
            when you
look
you cry//

shell
tower of pisa shard
lace
sandcastle
on pre-
sunset
western
sky

i stretch my hand
          to air

10/6

what passes for my
soot-charred brain
these days

have you been down
there, stench of
death &

heartbreak
scooping
the mash of civilization

& flesh, body
parts hanging
off girders

                              on chambers:
hand-written
sign: we're open

10/24: evening before my birthday

i've got lotsa
photos frm my west
window: water-
towers industrial funnels
bricks sky-splashed orange
neon liquors

at dusk but only one

frm the south
window the
second tower
falling, smoke,
memory, not one
of the Twins

& only one

of my
dad, i'm a baby
& he's holding me, lately
i've been thinking
of
leo:

firefighter, i am the
only daughter
of the
lion: for my sons
21st birthday
i give him

the shield

10/17: clinton towers

from
the window
on the 28th floor, waiting
for the elevator, looking at
the hudson, tiny wavelets, single
white ship navigating north,
appalachian foothills in jersey
misty
distance

i wanta get away
then see   the place
i wanna get away to
is here

3 a.m.

praying for snow
enuf to dust
manhattan, the
marble towers,
stars & juggernaut
of heaven

my mom

survived
the Depression &
WW2, my dad in
5 day coma
off a pier
fire, my dad
beating

her, my mom
survived
the Blacklist,
death of second
husband, close
friend, friends,
9/11

but, in
her single
bed at
Calvary, switched
from the
news
to Charlie

Rose, blue at the imminent
scimitar, yes, but terrified by Bush

lady vermeer
in memory of doris, my mom

can't sing a lick,
do the rhumba, cha-cha
& is definitely not
a lindy hopper

nor can she cook
good tho
turns out a mean
chicken soup

& she isn't
into xmas, new years,
birth-, emphatically not
mothers day

nor does she wrap gifts,

but
when the sun
beams thru
her red

hair, blue
hawk eye, gleams on
earring, thru
moving

hand, finger
brush, touches
paper, she is
alchemists

mistress, lady
vermeer,

pure

light

Eve Packer, Bronx-born, a graduate of the University of Michigan, attended Girton College, Cambridge, and received degrees from London School of Economics & NYU. She has traveled extensively in Europe and Latin America, taught at Queens College, the New School, local 1199, and is a Home Instruction teacher. An actress for many years, then performance artist and poet, she has been awarded grants from the New York State Council on the Arts, Jerome and Puffin Foundations, New York Foundation for the Arts (Poetry), a National Endowment for the Humanities to study classic lyric at Harvard, two *Downtown* Poet of the Year Awards, and a *Time to Consider: the Arts Respond to 9/11* Award.

She has studied poetry, classic and modern, with Gregory Nagy and Donald Hall. Appearing on stage with poets from Sapphire to Pedro Pietri to Allen Ginsberg, and in plays by Baraka and Beckett. As a performance artist she trained at Studio ReCherche with Ruth Malazcech and Lee Breuer, and has performed with musicians including Daniel Carter, Wilber Morris and Noah Howard.

She has appeared in numerous publications including *Long Shot, Tribes, Hart, Ikon, Cafe Review, Poetry in Performance*, and has performed at many venues including the Knitting Factory, Roulette, Bowery Poetry Club, Nuyorican Poets Cafe, Silver Arts Cultural Center, and Grounds for Sculpture.

With four chapbooks, her first book, *skulls head samba*, is also from *Fly By Night* Press. In addition she has two single and three long-playing poetry/jazz CD's (w/ Noah Howard): the long-playing *west frm 42nd, cruisin' w/moxie* (Altsax, Northcountry), and *that look* (Boxholder), and the single CDs: *ny woman* and *window:9/11* (Altsax, Northcountry). She co-ordinates a loose collective of poet/artists, *What Happens Next*.

She lives downtown, has a son, and swims daily.

Feisty little blond woman. Big Heart. Bigger Soul. Tough skin.Tough tears. Packer cruises thru the Word w/moxie. afire with the heat of a crazed & jittery Friday afternoon...that covers the continents from Africa to Nuyorico. From the depths & horrors of *love* to its ultimate joys, heights, disappointments, heartaches & anxieties. She delivers the *daily news* and *the advantage* of glimpsing a telling woman's heart. Heart of city of world. She tells it & tells it..as it is..& it should be...separates true & false... fact & fiction...lie..& yes shows us that truth is stranger...

Her empathy & compassion for humanity never comes thru stronger than in her *window:9/11* poems. I had the privilege of hearing these pieces the very first time Packer read them in public a short while after 9/11 on a sunny afternoon in the garden of Steve Cannon & A Gathering of Tribes, the first afternoon, when many of us who lived thru 9/11 & who live in the downtown area, got to hear birds singing again since that awe-filled day.

These poems depict a truly individual approach to that touchy subject as well as zeroing in on the uniqueness of the individual during that trying time when Packer herself managed to 'volunteer' her way into St. Vincent's hospital where she answered phones.. Hence sad Amaryllis..so real so strong yet so much like a shadow.. & the birds where have the birds gone? left town with their songs under wing? Packer makes us relive 9-ll not with the overwhelming sentimentality that America has fallen prey to but with true grace, dignity & eye-opening triste.

What is Love? It's an unbreakable heart. A heart easily broken. It's everything here in these poems. Hold them. Be TOUCHED.

— *steve dalachinsky*
nycptt 3a.m. 2/23/03

Praise for these poems

Michael Basinski: "Eve Packer's voice is a velvet night...
steaming streets and subways, canyons between buildings
and sirens, Hudson & East River. She is a Siren..."

Dennis Duggan (*Newsday*): "... a woman of talent, imagination,
and a mind that engages you in ways you seldom
encounter...offbeat, amusing, witty and sweet..smokey & sexy
in a way that makes you think of love."

Scott Morgan: "...recorder, observer, poet...lyricist & stop-
watch. Wide-angle lens & Polaroid. The metaphor to describe
Eve Packer today is the subway, a juggernaut that is both
conduit & passerby; a surrreal underworld where life's rhythms
take you far away but always bring you home...Life at the speed
of life..."

Frank Rubolino: "...a woman of our times..profound..eloquent
simplicity blanketed by soul... hip..flowing..sensual..astute..."

David Lewis: "...sassy, confident..contemporary, street smart,
combining raw urban perceptions with sensitivity to the human
condition...I was charmed & moved by an honest document of
the post 9/ll era."